MW01108338

"*Stories Dreamed* is a magnificent journey into that place where time slips into eternity...With the eye of a naturalist and the heart of a mystic, Abel deftly guides the reader into a landscape which becomes dreamscape with only a shimmering, translucent veil between them...."
  --YOGACHARYA ELLEN GRACE O'BRIAN, author of *The Moon Reminded Me*

"While Wallace Stevens once famously placed a jar and watched the landscape rise up around it, Walker Abel has placed himself among mountains and rivers, beaches and forests. His poetic sensibility adds life to their life..."
  --MIRIAM SAGAN, author of *Love and Death: Greatest Hits* and *Black Rainbow*

"Walker Abel's delicate poems are like carefully held embers carried across time and space. Each one suffused with a haunting sense of distance and yearning, yet twined with Abel's rapt attention for silent heartbeats that only owls hear and bent grasses left by passing deer. These are poems that illuminate and fill the wild, living places out of which they were born."
  --DAVID LUKAS, author of *Language Making Nature* and *Sierra Nevada Birds*

Stories Dreamed
from Dust *and* Distant Light

Stories Dreamed
from Dust *and* Distant Light

WALKER ABEL

HOMEBOUND
PUBLICATIONS

Published in 2017 • Homebound Publications
Front Cover Image © Rudy Balasko
Cover and Interior Designed by Leslie M. Browning
ISBN • 978-1-947003-70-5
First Edition Trade Paperback

Homebound Publications
Ensuring the mainstream isn't the only stream.
WWW.HOMEBOUNDPUBLICATIONS.COM

10 9 8 7 6 5 4 3 2 1

Homebound Publications is committed to ecological stewardship. We greatly value the natural environment and invest in environmental conservation. Our books are printed on paper with chain of custody certification from the Forest Stewardship Council, Sustainable Forestry Initiative, and the Program for the Endorsement of Forest Certification.

Dedication

"The press of my foot to the earth
springs a hundred affections...."
–Walt Whitman

This book is dedicated to the many college students through 28
years of teaching with whom I had the great good fortune to
share a semester backpacking and camping together while dis-
cussing environmental literature and ecopsychology.

And dedicated also, and especially!, to the many wild places
we went, and for a time, lived with.

Foreword

It is not as easy at it seems to really connect at psychological levels with those wild remnants of nature we term "wilderness". It is even more difficult to express such connections in words without seeming maudlin or without trivializing the experience. Few have been able to do so—Gary Snyder, Mary Oliver, Richard Nelson. Now Walker Abel, author of this exquisite collection of poems, takes his place among them.

For 25 years at Sonoma State University, I taught a course entitled "The Experience of Wilderness". This class was an early exploration into what has come to be known as "ecopsychology", a field of study which in general I think of as inquiry into the human/nature relationship—what cultural and psychological qualities make that relationship healthy, what make it problematic. In what we might call "lab work", this class included two and three-week trips into wildernesses. That is where the real depth occurred. Walker came along in the mid-1980s, and I soon realized that as a professor, I had in him that rare delight: a student who becomes as much a teacher as a learner, a source of wisdom into my own work, and even a life-long friend.

So here are Walker's words about "the experience of nature", so much of it drawn from his almost three decades of experience leading his own environmental studies field programs through the Sierra Institute, located out of UC/Santa Cruz and later UC/Davis. Under that auspice, he became a much loved teacher—students would learn through Walker's patient guidance to approach wilderness as lover rather than as conquistador, colonist, or walking embodiment of an outfitters' catalogue. "Leave no trace" of our visits, he taught, knowing that traces of "the experience of wilderness" would remain with us for the rest of our lives.

These poems emerge from those wilderness traces, but they do so without ignoring the deep paradox within which we all live—that wildness is not exclusive to remote regions, that remnants of "the natural" reside full time in our bodies, gardens, intimacy with weather, fondness for national parks, longing glances at distant sceneries. The paradox of ever-present wildness is with us even while we shop for food at supermarkets (products shipped from thousands of miles away), order entertainment and arrange human encounters via computers we carry in our pockets, while we race around behind the power of hundreds of horses, fueled by burning the residue of ancient life.

My personal and academic interests have always converged around ideas (and ever-evolving theories!) about the possibilities and range of deep human connection to the earth. This requires examining issues around dualism and non-dualism, around an isolated self versus an intersubjective ecological self, and issues around what we might call the "front-country" mind versus a "back-country" mind, in which human-centeredness is perhaps dispersed into a much larger encompassing field of nature and being.

Though I have loved my decades of intellectual engagement with ecopsychology, the theory has always been balanced with experiential knowing. In other words, I've favored theory that includes experience—even the ineffable aspects of experience, or at least the expression of experience requiring a subtle and nuanced language. I've found such language in various realms of psychology (especially Jung), philosophy (especially Whitehead and Wilber) and ecology (especially Bateson, both Gregory and Nora). But the method and music of poetry has always been another language drawing me as well—and thus Walker's beautiful embodiment of this approach enriches the ecopsychology that I have tried to "know" and express.

Poetry uses flashes of image, and counts on the simple resonance we feel with them, in Walker's words, "From the lake/ you step wet and clean/ blue birth/ of a marmot whistle..." The poem "Night Flooding a Mountain Valley" begins "Setting sun ebbs on eastern slope/ and line of shadow rises like dark water/ forcing forms of day to go under." Or, "Every moment's a gamble/ we lose the sun and gain the moon./ Maybe one stiff drink of night stars/ will steady our bet". Through these and much more, Walker gives us "nature" in a world hell-bent to destroy it.

And so—read this book! Take it out on a hike with you. Note the intertwining of the erotic with the natural—and feel the "of course", that an integration with nature does not depend on technological fixes, and that to counter the grief that so many of us feel at the rapidly increasing environmental crisis, at the loss of the natural, we can arm ourselves with our own homage to "the forgotten things" —the sounds and scents of night winds, the flash of native trout in mountain pools, sun-warmed boulders, wisps of clouds rushing past mountain outcroppings.

I see these poems as an exquisite and poignant guide to the natural world that still can inform us, that resonates with our own remnant naturalness.

Deep gratitude, Walker, for these experiences, so richly shared.

–Robert Greenway
Corona Farm, Port Townsend, Washington
Spring 2017

Contents

I

Encounter

Everything we live
lived elsewhere once.
Falls into our lap
out of that nothing.
The black bird
lays a speckled egg
and mountains hatch.
Bits of shell
still dot your hair.
From the lake
you step wet and clean
blue birth
of a marmot whistle.
Moments this dark
shine silver
when the sun angles.
I could swim
the invisible
and never come up
but I'd miss
when the moment's face
is yours
turning toward me.

Well Met

If she meets you in meadow
watch the way her feet bend grass
and if stalks lean primarily west
go that way because it's favorable
and look at nothing too closely
but listen for the story
her moving legs tell
from inside everything.

If passing the redwood she pauses
to let fingertips like raindrops
trace down textures of trunk
then taking no steps
intending no future
drink that glistening water
before her touch dries.

And now lose feet
downward into depth
and from top of head
feel lost into lift
because the world in its middle
can break open

the startled deer will bound
and if you exclaim
look an arc of glory in its leap
then that is favorable
because she knows at last
that she and another
are celebrating the same earth.

Behind this Ocean

Behind this ocean is another ocean
with its own shores and fires and people dancing.
Behind this tree, another forest begins.
There are swallows over the river
that cast shadows on grey stones.
When deer wade across
their slender shins drip water.
Take now the ocean, take now the forest
take the swallows, river, deer.
Place them behind your eyes
and let me look at you.
Everything is shining on the shore
where it has always been.

She Said

She said she could hear the rocks singing
as she walked the dry riverbed. Later
she told me it would rain in three days
which it did, and we watched the river
begin seasonal return. One day under cedar
she held my hand, and hers was like a leaf
and like a mountain and like all the various winds
that close to ground swirl forest duff.
When she left she took an ember from our fire
wrapped it in leaves and ash saying she would
start another from it and from that another
so on down river all the way to sea.
I think about the foggy coast, how the gulls
must have parted as she crossed the beach
how she threw the final ember into waves.
Don't know if she went north or south after that
shouldering a blanket and not much else.
There are angry men on the roads
hungry for a love they don't know how to feel.
When I break this camp, I'll carry an ember
far as it takes to burn this clench from fist.

Grace

Three days under trees he lay alone and healed.
Twenty years later saying grace at meal
remembered that fragrance of sycamore and fern.
All hands were clasped, heads bowed save one
young girl who looked with unshadowed eye.
She saw the wound like a swan at gloaming.

Said of her ever afterwards she could eat no food
without first letting arms settle slowly to sides.
Doesn't take long that gesture.
Passerby out window will think nothing
just old woman alone with candlelit meal
and a stately motion like fold of white wings.

Just a random sight falling away with other randoms.
Then the passerby would be gone, his footsteps
echoing down flagstone walk to another house
opening its door into familiar light, his children
already seated at table with heads bowed
for the grace he is suddenly too inundated to utter.

Owl

There was a day before the dogwood bloomed
when forest hid in its own silence like closed hand.
Mantling herds of cloud moved over face of sky.
You went to the spring with cup of hollowed wood
and stood before water through season of mind.
I did not ask for story though looked
to downcast eyes of small flowers
that bloomed in damp among moss and fern.
Could hear nothing, not wind or river
not breath or heartbeat but still
your head like owl tilted toward distant sound.

Stone

He carried a stone in pocket
so dark no one could see
though its shadow
chased him sometimes
on days he did not mean to fear.
So weightless it seemed
to float him above river
but drowning was something
he convinced was shore.
Showed once to woman
who cried three days
then parceled out as rain.
Toweling dry
he found the stone
blinking ruby and lapis
like a star just surfacing
from hiddenmost horizon of her skin.

Implausible

You are lost to me now in river of sands
as sound might be lost that was sung once
in green recess of trees, then vanished there
unfollowable—and yet not so remote
as not yet still to be felt
in some strand of my knowing—

your very distance has become your closeness
your absence ... your presence
you are with me now
as you could never be if you were simply here.

Through all these desert days
some part of me holds
to the green tendril of your song
fragile and translucent, implausible
twining as it does further and further away
inaccessible and safe, alive there forever
as my lonely fingers
touched to your untouchable wrist
divine you to be.

Night Flooding a Mountain Valley

Setting sun ebbs on eastern slope
and line of shadow rises like dark water
forcing forms of day to go under.

I will sleep, I will dream
I will drift down as creature
browsing sunken architecture of ship.

No one knows when it sailed or on what oceans.
It has cabins, corridors
metal-hinged chests dagger-locked.

Some say moon lost inamorato
on that ship—swept sudden
when mutinous wave broke over bow.

Again and again from heaving froth he called
but course was set and her knuckles
gripped white the gunwales of stern.

In pale morning she went below
lifted his shirt from the heaven of bed
hung it in dark confine of closet.

If dreaming ever bring you to that ship
beware the smell of spices, beware
the glimpse of her shimmering leg.

And pray thee note the scattered skeletons
of them who sought that inmost bed
fancied they could don that smoldering shirt.

Reckless

Reasons to cry will always
slide down stems of plants
as though the light that shines
answers to earth's thirst.
Like grazing animals
some sadness never leaves
this field of green
rooted as it is in aromatic rot
of clouds and leaves.
You have lain in places
where I have never wept.
If told now I had three years
I would lace them round your ankle
and follow where you tiptoe
along the edge of bearing.

River

The river winds toward a nearness I cannot name
not even at night when icicles jangle on stems of willow
and my heart goes naked as the grief-bones of an ancestor dance.

The river seen from above and the whistle of wings in my ear
distance circling back, no telling snowfield from sea
all curled like a dreamed animal nose to tail
and time sleeping warm as the color of its fur.

Your body in the river as though made of moonlight
slippery as melon, ethereal as chorus out of water sound
your hair floats like nets of welcome
and no part of your being is not inclusive of mine or the river's.

Every Moment

This shade of moving tree—
how it hovers on cusp
of what has never been.

A rider comes over hill, dismounts.
Throws three gold coins on table.
One spins on edge:
yellow hills of grass
turning in the wind.

That's the coin that buys us—
a whole life laid down
like deck of cards to seasons.

Every moment's a gamble.
We lose the sun and gain the moon.
Maybe one stiff drink of night stars
will steady our bet.

Like the saloon girl
petticoat slung from branch by river.
Under tree of moving shade
horses graze, and the day's earnings
cast to nothing in her gaze.

Sliver Moon on Lost Coast

Last night, a russet-flanked bull
big-shouldered and slow
waded along western edge of sea.

I vaulted its gate of horn
to a place that was burnished and bright—
we were walking past kelp-draped rocks
the whiskered heads of seals
watched while gulls wheeled down.
Our hands were light as driftwood
come to rest in upland grass.

You said to fill seven hoof marks
with pledges of seven griefs
then lay myself down—split cloud
on the absolving body of that beach.

I drifted then like prayer smoke
out over the days of the world
drawn with tidal foam toward sunset edge—
that tumbling brink, that tender shore
where light goes under
finds depth in your fathoms of dark.

Sunken Forests

She said she could feel her hands
dangling in dark waters, sunken forests.
Shapes down there to only describe
by letting voice fall blind into the hole
that tunnels endless where fear starts.
One day she lifted up arms
and shreds so green as almost to be black
clung to crevices between fingers.
An earth wind shook upwards
and something like birds splattered into air.
I thought I could hear the ocean then
but I'm sure it was just that her toenails
looked like shells, and her face
like backlit clouds of storm
that long ago washed them inland.

This Morning

Like flecks of dust small birds filter through trees
a song glinting from each beak.
Often the sieve of attention lets the little things pass.
But they rain down soft as fingers, find the spot
where on foggy day sorrow was buried.

The ocean rolls large stones yet grains of sand
are its gift to the wind. When the princess
sets up pavilion on sea-scoured bluff
everyone looks to horizon while unseen
she ducks out back, meets her lover
among forgotten stalks of autumn grass.

He kisses her lips encompassing as a world
but it's tiniest tip of her tongue
that opens him to love's flavor.
Now he'll walk on back trails, lost twilights
while out in open fields stream her noon-high pennants.

Think of the miners who swirled pans for sturdy nuggets
while all the rest was sloshed away.
But a seamstress downriver saw what was passing
threw in cloth to dye her apron gold.

Somewhere nearby under weight of winter vines
sags her front porch. But go around back
and they say she bakes thimble-sized muffins
and barefoot serves from shimmering tray.

Wild Azalea

I slept all night in scent of azalea
and woke wrapped and tangled in that long hair.
Syrupy scent of azalea
smooth as oiled skin.
From under lace canopy, dangling a leg—
white blossom of calf and thigh
blush of pink.
Oh the tireless river
cool hands over the arching body of earth
gripping the curve of waist
bending to the scent of azalea.
I slept all night on a river terrace
and woke among temple columns of sugar pine and cedar
open-robed azalea still ministering from bed to bed.

The Woman Who Married a Bear

Once it seems there was light
off morning leaves, there was
birdsong at dusk, the moon walked
as you did, with ankle bells
and cloths of grey and silver.
There were winds, fields
flowered bends of small creeks.
You went out one morning
to gather berries, and never
returned, or was it me
who heard at night
something moving on the mountain
and knew it as myself?
Yes, you went for berries
that was it
the simple red ones
close to earth
the finger-staining ones
black among thorns.
I heard something on mountain
rolled toward it under stars
your sleeping hand fell slowly
from the heartbeat of my chest.
Tell me soon when you have found
your berries of light.
Bring them ripe. Marry
this darkness with their taste.

The End of Nature

Once between then and forever
the dogwood blossom passed out of knowledge
like sea foam escorted by night currents
and whether by deprivations or extravagances
no one noticed but kept on in their ways
in which the white petals poised unassuming
on forested hillsides did not play part
and no one no longer commended them
with eyes and touch so they were left
to guard within themselves their own quintessence
yet one woman on the dark shore threw out nets for sea foam
her house of driftwood refuged the forgotten things
though she herself was such, choosing long nights
with the vanishing tides and wondering whether
there were any words other than ones for farewell.

Corridors

Once within corridors of water and stone
where wind, where leaves
spin a thousand worlds in eddy of each sensation
you stood in your own raiment among bones
a horizon that the drum of earth bears upward into beauty.
Face covered in ash I slipped along lines of shadow
while insinuations of light
prompted forest into music of mist and cedar bark.
Something swirling slings forth a panoply of places.
Shape and shapeless saturate maelstrom of depth.
These oak leaves of spring so articulate and frail
are breath feathers that birth in a windstorm
navigate the same doom and glory that blasts sentience
and breaks it like sparking rocks on mountain.
And all for melodies, all for the coy girl dancing behind tree
for the cascading field of green that rips its heart open
so you step out singing the name you called me once
as you pierced your own body with incantations and jewels.
That was ages ago and yet still to be.
I can't tell your eyes from clouds or rain from prophesy.

Cottonwood

Once the yellowed leaf of a cottonwood
fell in the river, and bird on limb
watched the leaf float
because nothing more
in that moment and nothing less
a great equality suffusing
world of tree and moving water.
When woman wades in
sunning turtle dives for bottom.
She doesn't mean to scare. Nothing
in the intertwining can ever burden.
One morning she learned
to love deeper than leaf
or its shadow on river bottom.
Then bird lifted from branch
taking yellow of cottonwood
and twining it rapt
in colorless cloud of her gaze.

Desert Night

Once in desert night rain fell so softly
it dried as it hit rocks, shrubs
the eyelids of a sleeping man.
He woke nevertheless to that truth.
One raindrop is the fall of freedom
and a thousand make a veil
behind which lovers get married.
At dawn he will watch curtains of rain
pass silken over distant slopes.
There will be other weddings.
The touch of love is like that
waking in desert night
when owls are calling.
At first light they melt
into darkness of canyon trees.
Their brush of wing bends air
and it is night again, raining.

Field of Lupine

Once rain fell onto field of lupine
and whoever walked through
turned into something they already were
but had forgotten, as though long ago
stepped into that other
while the original had kept going

parallel, not far, and watched the other
as we might a fish in clear aquarium
swimming amid strands of weed
and so it went till the rain and lupine
brought the wandering life to back door
unmarked and invisible as it is
not even there they say, thus unfindable
and anyone observing from edge

would have seen nothing unusual
just someone walking through flowered field
getting wet from above and below
and yet maybe the whole scene
                    reminiscent of empty aquarium
                    and strangely of a piece as seeing is.

Flash

Once he saw flash in pool of water
a face not his own or any that he knew
though afterwards it stayed with him
a wetness on skin that would not dry.
Made fire one night in circle of trees
face flamed for moment then hid in shadow
went wandering, lost into canyon rock.
Water summons its own and they go
all the way to moss and unlit drip
first seep in cleft of mountain.
There he fit one finger and touched
on eyes of blind one that sees.

Once the Water

Once the water moved more slowly than now
and there was time on river banks to watch
how it curled around itself, lifted and fell.
Even the light was different then
both the sun striding in sovereign mantle
and the moon patient in grey feathers.
We knew the winds well, they like water
stayed near us, cradled our company.
The trees, they spoke more, were looser of limb
and in wind-sway they ushered us back
to a yet more distant time slower still
but one we could dream of then
if we washed our roots in river
and laid our tendrils on warmth of stone.
But those dreams are gone from us now
though we wake in sense of their shape and shadow
to watch mergansers fly over the river course
deep in the sleep of what we can't remember.

Sea Winds

Once I could hear on sea winds
something shaped like the inside of shells
could be led down pearl corridors
fingers of sense sliding on smooth walls
down in spirals it seemed
until a silence opened around me

and I could see the tuft
of each grass head bobbing
which together made the motion of the meadow
and which I knew then was also the motion
of the sea I was born in long ago
newly returned, never left
not a thing anywhere moving
yet the grass tufts bobbed
and the sea winds blew.

Tree Rings

Once under oak a life was laid bare to heart
concentric impress of sun and stars peeled back
and beyond them even to what
had never yet happened and couldn't happen
because composed of the unborn dark
beneath sprout of farthest root tip.
And so the life passed into no hands
but stayed where it was, sensing something
like the press of loneliness
before loneliness knows it is lonely.

Over There

Once I found my ears
strangely listening
to the other side of the river
as though I were
over there
among its trees
the looming rocks
of its canyon wall.
The sounds were language
like someone else's toes
on my feet. Leaf touch
was cold on skin
fingers of an echo.
I walked for time
that left little mark
but look now across water
and glimpses of my own steps
is what I hear.

Once a Wind

Once a wind passed through a dell
and what was with that wind
was never again after
though she went looking through years
and thought she saw a time or two
vaguely as behind tree limbs just leafing out
or like tail of animal while body
and bright face are already hidden.

And so she went on with memory of wind
she went on and came at night to river-crossing—
high water and among dark boulders
a tumble of white. When morning came
she was nowhere she knew
though above in trees wind moved.

She sensed it again many years later
picnic of coleslaw, egg salad
and the eyes of the woman watched
the child's hair wave in wind.
Afternoon brought rain. They found
old farm shed where child napped while
woman walked among apples long unattended

and thought of nothing that wasn't
already being sung by light
how it found its way through clouds

down even to her toes, the flowers
the wooden fence posts, down also
to the basket that later she carried
in one hand, child holding her other.

Bird Fish

Once a bird flew over mountain lake
raven of black wing, shiny eye
casting shadow that across water
raced silver, but not so swift
as not to be caught. Splash of large fish
pulled it down to eat at depth.
Then to its scales came gradually
a shine, such that in shallows by moonlight
the fish appeared pearly and luminescent
a buoyant glow just below the surface
that the raven, mystified
would come to lake's edge to watch.

III

Antler and Acorn

Deer antler and acorn, so little to find on ground
yet full import of world spills out
just as river of autumn through escort of boulders
is cast from what cannot be seen.

Everything made of empty arms of moment
crevices only fingers released into death can feel
not cold death but the other one, the death
running now through dry grass under trees
branches whipping moon like a sickle.

A hot running, a can't-get-enough running
and all the while by the river
alder leaves reflect green and brown in a pool
and I would look through that eye to see
an acorn that fell, an antler that fell
a night that fell through birth veils of oblivion
to die running in a morning that never wasn't.

Chestnut and Honey

The bird flew into his mouth
as though it were the opening of a cave
circled three times round the first chamber
before dropping into the second and third
then plunged down swiftly and finally
out through the bottom of his foot.

And he could see all the root hairs of the trees
lit for that instant like lightning
and then he was standing again, in daylight
the lingering leaves of the aspen were yellow
though the last season he could remember was spring

and when he coughed, a single feather
the color of chestnut and honey
issued into the air, and he followed it
because that was simplest, and he liked
how it wafted through first falling snow.

Autumn Leaves

But on these days there was for him
the impression of weightlessness or clairvoyance
that accompanies mornings under autumn oaks
how breezes come through
more impossibly invisible than they already are
so much so that he could not fetter the instant
but felt it pulled like taffy in all directions
and it calmed him but also had stirrings of force
the way tree rings do around their core
and still there were intimations he could not name
some of it had to do with smallness
of his hands, say, as he held them between body and sky
of hopes that seemed unnecessary now
superfluous even in the abundance of leaves
that he knew would fall steadily about him
so that throughout his later years
his love would say that in his walking
there was always the company of a rustling sound
as though ankle deep in leaves of tan and yellow.

Old Man on Lost Coast

Walking those years in silence
old man on the bluffs
staff thumping the rocks
thumping the meadows of lupine and poppy
thumping the winter rains
old man, hair like spider threads
collecting beads of fog.

All those years of silence
strung together like pelicans in a chain
one smooth and dreamy glide
going on, going on.

Voice hidden as a clam's foot
voice recalcitrant
voice at last a curl of driftwood
sun and salt bleached

a curving shell, a spiral hollow
picked up, held to ear
and all the susurrus of sea
like faithful blood
singing the lost body of mortality.

Loon

Three gulls
flew into fog and faded.
The rest is unknown.

Undercurrents of ocean
cast up
broken shells of all outcomes.

A man paints his face with ash
hunkers down amid driftwood.
When at last he calls
song out of sea
it comes already
scarred, bitten
crusted in barnacle.

But buried deep in sand
lies urn of wave and wing.
Fell from ship long ago
floated dark fortnights
till foundering on shore.

Now it mumbles
like pebbles slurring
says the spell that foreshadows
where the loon that dove
will of a sudden reappear.

Autumn Aspen Grove

I was here before I was born
and before I was born
autumn light in aspen grove
was on my feet and turned me
in a dance of green and yellow.

Round I went in the light
and the water of falling yellow
carried me .... round I went
in the autumn grove
dissolved in sea of green and yellow.

I was here before I was born
yet being born and past born
still here ... turning, turning
untethered, free
spun as swirls
of aspen green and yellow.

While I Go

I want to swim across the lake using only wings that grew
between evening when you kissed me and morning
when your feet made small path through grass.

I want to die with back upon rock and sky forthright
as waterfall pounding. To know one thing clear
as pine needle, listen to it in wind when geese are flying.

Want to cover myself in blanket of leaves till hands
more translucent than touch lift me to river
and all my selves are bank-side fronds waving while I go.

Desert Thoughts

Clouds cool the desert air
and rest is taken under trees
while wild horses move
with their own breed of thought
more amorphous, I imagine, than mine
rounded and soft-edged
drifting in vague directions
as people seem to
when viewed from height of years
like someone a century or two ago
finding surface sign of turquoise
digging out with pick and shovel
loading mule for transport
a dozen years perhaps
but the worn track of that coming and going
now long lost, faded to nothing
by wind-blow of sands and gravels.
The miner gone too, absent even
to thin branches of remembered genealogy
while on most days
active or paused
in sun or shade
his thoughts never knew
they were following each other
nose to tail
toward this type of extinction.

Original Face

I was crossing then streams
crossed before, but long ago
so that seeing them now was different
nothing in particular known
but in the whole familiar—
damp rocks, oaks and bays
a certain curve and fall to the water—
this journey on trails
made of such moments—
the paths crisscross, double-back
splice and tear away
we are gone as we arrive
arrive as we are gone.
Through green turnings
sudden storm fronts
we love in loneliness
in loneliness, love.
The way weaves strands
sways like head of hair in water
and a face comes up
haloed in droplets
doesn't look toward you
because you're looking as it.

In the End

In the end it was not fever
or snakebite or rock fall
nothing but the passage of time
which by then seemed nothing at all
not even the gauziest snakeskin
to hold between fingertips to heaven.
And lying there in bed
he gazed to right of window
where hung driftwood-framed
the watercolor of anonymous years:
cabin on grassy coast with lupine and poppy
the blue and white of the world
that had seemed in the painter's gaze
to be something stout, steadfast
and not something ostensible
as the number of sheddings a snake will believe
before its entirety is translucent and gone.

Inyo Range

Couldn't tell where I was today—
bird blown beyond boundaries.
Place was treeless. Formations of rock
reared as carved fetishes—
stern forearms and fierce glares
bearing down on the small babe of the world.
When clouds cracked open into light
hoofed creatures ran from that fissure with flame.

Out on alpine flats, something was crying
and I was close enough to run through that rain
as though it were last judgment of my days.

Disclose where you are.
Be the thunder that trembles rocks
into breathing bodies, flings them earthward
writhing with the consequence of blood.

Lantern

If I left now to cross at run
this desert flat tonight
I might be early.
But if I wait, I may never see
the small light again
or how so frail
it picks its winding way.
I know the night is long and legs get weary.
I know I was last heard
loping between brittle clumps of shrub.
Made of moon and rock
I know there are birds
that sing without opening their beaks.

Late Night

It is night. Late. Not far from morning really.
The owl says nothing I haven't a thousand times
said myself, as though the stars above the trees
spoke feathers through me, the ones that prove

distance falls to nothing, less than ash
at end of campfire, while frogs thigh-deep
keep throating through the melted snows of spring
and bear tracks dented into forest duff

go round and round the weightless crux
my body rests upon. I can feel
the rhythm of acorns cracked in stone mortar
feel the shins of deer brush across meadow grass

while dogwoods open into rafts of flower
that float like mist above a river. Floating, floating
eyes close into sleep or death, and all the seasons find themselves
back in their own company before the mountain was made.

Sixty Years

Something draws me again and again
into frailty of moment
where early morning
it squats by ring of stone
uses breath to raise
flame from ember.

First plume of wispy smoke
drifts off
through drowse of cedar.

Warming hands, what puzzles
is absolute absence
of yesterday
of last year's leaves of summer
of any glade I walked through
as though that shared body of instance
had been more
than parlor trick of time and light.

Yet something is the same today
as any hour ever
something absolute in me
unaltered through years of aging.

Now I am drawn again and again
into durable moment
the yellow flames that effortlessly persist
the one fire that does not move
though it burn all content
without smoke, ash, or concern.

Meadows Above Sea

These moonlight walks in meadows above the sea
grasses standing yellow and pale as brimming beer
old men with knobby hands
drink it warm, draughts hefty with foam
well-flavored in barrels
crafted from wave and rumbling cobble.

Comfortable as driftwood settling into sand
they tell stories of sea birds and whales
of migrations, crossings, the slow swimming
of continents and change.

Later they sing—
songs out of the deep
kelp-covered, barnacled.
Later still they grow quiet
hands of fog drifting to bellies
eyes far off and slivered
like horizon, a trace of glow.

Dawn comes long-haired and skirted.
She sweeps, arranges chairs
blush-cheeked swishes through the familiar crowd
gently rouses each groggy man just enough
to point his shuffling way home.

Salvation

Salvation, I'm sure, has a salty taste.
It must also be bottomed with ships
that sank with sails at full-mast.
Such are the ways of wind
they bend compass beyond bearing.
Yet over horizonless waters
the processional flight of gulls
shines like flowered wreath
tossed to weary wake.
Beauty floats in air or sea
but pushed on land it stumbles.
Build me a house of driftwood
and I will stay three days.
After that the house of waves
is my only heaven
and blue and white
the one wreath I can endure.

Shimmy

Birds were moving between nests of shadow.
A rustle of memory, a softness of twilight
brown patterns redolent of wing and dark eye.

Tumult in the air as well, one season of knowledge
shifting weight to another, while mountain gathered mist
rolled it between forested arms without effort

without indication of intent, a murmur spreading
through canopy that I could not precisely hear
yet all leaves ushered it with green innuendo.

And as sudden, you were there, walking in rain
garment of sheen as though shimmied out of old skin
and left in litter what once had been everything.

Silver Water of the Desert

Occurrence lays over me like silver water
and I cannot remember
what anything may have been
before it is what it is now.
Something always something
calling in faint voice
a small bird maybe
veiled in tangle of brush
a young girl before the advent of worry.
Her shining anklet
rings bell-like out of nothing
bare steps are trackless days
losing boundary in expanse of summer.
Gone, always gone, but now
sunlight is white on stricken stalks
and it seems all things must turn
upon themselves to discover
they birth and die
in the unborn spill of silver water.

Story for the Boys

We go out and wander the meadows and hills.
That is our way. But always
we come back to this circle of trees.

Try some night to stay away
point your spear and run, like the hunters
who followed the bear over hill after hill
and finally right up into the sky.

But you will find these meadows twist
the ravines spiral; strive as you will
the land brings you back again and again.

You will enter there
run three times round the inner circle
then give your accounting.
That is our way.
Pant with coyote down the long trail
stay with the scents and markers
keep distant rumble of surf on your left, and go
go...go...go.

But on some contour, and in full stride
suddenly the trees again
their bulky shapes rising out of nowhere
massive trunks capped like mushrooms
far spreading limb, dense drooping canopy.

You will enter there, through the dark passage
and run three times round the inner circle.
You must run with high drawn knees
three times while the old women watch.
Then point your spear at the hunters turned stars
then plant it in the earth.

Now the old women will listen to your accounting.
And then as always, they will send you out
with a tendril so thin, you, as always, forget
until like spiders they reel you back
the dark web of interlacing leaves
the sticky gaze of their wrinkled faces.

One day, in open meadow
you will behold the endless thrust of bright chested color
as rank after rank of small bird
throw songs like spears
into swallowing space of sky.
That is our way.

And one night, moon or no moon
the abiding circle will close
the old women devour you.

Terma in White Mountains

After passing rain
thigh-high sagebrush
startles into fragrance.

Then between thunderhead clouds
a chasm of blue—
one world plummets to another.

Came down chute of shale
shards sounding
whispered singing
old women
twisting fibers
out of cave smoke and starlit air.

At bottom—green grass, water
trout color of blood and twilight mixed
without hands or words
wafting in clean presence.

Virtues of Falling

If rain never fell there would be no utterance under oaks
to carry the refugee affections that raft
across estuaries of nostalgia and longing.

If moon never fell into sea there would be no waves
to wash with silver the off-shore rock
where roosts vagrant lovers counting rosaries of amends.

If in nights of desert-walking stars never fell
there would be no glimmer under impassive dust
that ambling steps of happenchance scuff to uncover.

If stones never fell from unity of mountain
then the fox would have nothing to chase
and tales of its golden speed would fallow and waste.

Then

Only then
did the scent of pine needles
encounter no edges.
It seemed not rare, those days.
Wind and a welcome.
When the moon walked
there was no wondering
how the fallen needles
felt so soft under foot.

Tindavar

Once a story was told that meant nothing
unless it were rainy day and dogwoods were in bloom
in which case it meant as much as everything
since everything was in it, down to the little spark
thrown from campfire that Tindavar caught in hand
and allowed to burn into him. It burrowed
like termite into wood, networks of lit tunnels
passages intertwined, linked, and he was all of them at once
world rushing into every space, painting itself in alcove
on ceiling, in niche ornate and intricate.
How a deer insouciant as dawn walked through
browsed on currant bush while of course a dogwood
bloomed nearby in rain so light, white petals hardly shook.
And so the story went on as stories do, more room
being made within to match pace without
till no one any longer could say who the teller
who the listener, or how it ever came to be
that into lucent fractals Tindavar still perfused.

Center of Experience

When you think, on those walks in the mountains
that the world is falling into your heart
like a snowflake into water, maybe
it's the crystalline edges of you
drifting down into the heart of the world.

You look around—nothing but blizzard.
Everything's falling
the trees, the rocks, the river
the juncos scattering from bush.
A storm of selves, you among them
falling and falling
flakes into indiscernible water
a heart you can't claim
to the small cavity of your chest.

Wild Iris

The petals of this wild iris
do not dissolve in rain
but tremble
like song of hermit thrush
tipping along edge
of what had been night
a song as small
as grip of the bird's toe
so small
eternity can't cover it
and nothing more need be said
of the iris and the rain
because the tongue exults
as it nears the petal
and confirms that darkness
is not annulled by light
nor love by absence
and assured at other edge
the unseen thrush
woodland-dressed
issues again
its song of petals and rain.

Between Now and My Death

Between now and my death is an ocean
blue and obliging to horizon unknown.
From out its waves an island calls
harboring a nest in cornice of stone.

Between now and my death I am flying
stalks of meadow grass treasured in hand.
Golden with dying earth are they
golden as dying sun on sand.

And I will lay the gold of what I am
to line the hollow of that island nest
and I will die as I have lived
a glint of gold flying to the west.

About the Author

Walker Abel, along with his partner Willow, lives at a remote off-grid home in northern California. As an undergraduate at University of California, Santa Cruz, Walker participated in an environmental studies field program called Sierra Institute. Twelve years later (1988), after completing a graduate degree with ecopsychology pioneer Robert Greenway, Walker came back to UCSC to teach for Sierra Institute, which he did for 28 years, while also taking on the role of director in 2003. Most of his poetry has been written in field journals while out on these 9-week academic programs, which were taught entirely off-campus during a series of backpacking trips in wild areas of California. One of his greatest joys was watching each new group of students open over time to the transformative influence of wilderness immersion.

Walker's first book, *The Uncallused Hand*, won the 2014 Poetry Prize from Homebound Publications. That book also went on to be a Finalist in *Foreword Reviews* 2014 Book of the Year and to win Gold in the 2015 Nautilus Awards.

Walker has practiced Zen with Roshis John Tarrant and David Weinstein of Pacific Zen Institute, and is currently a student of Roshi Teja Bell of Qigong Dharma.

HOMEBOUND
PUBLICATIONS

Ensuring that the mainstream isn't the only stream.

At Homebound Publications, we publish books written by independent voices for independent minds. Our books focus on a return to simplicity and balance, connection to the earth and each other, and the search for meaning and authenticity. Founded in 2011, Homebound Publications is one of the rising independent publishers in the country. Collectively through our imprints, we publish between fifteen to twenty offerings each year. Our authors have received dozens of awards, including: *Foreword Reviews'* Book of the Year, Nautilus Book Award, Benjamin Franklin Book Awards, and Saltire Literary Awards. Highly-respected among bookstores, readers and authors alike, Homebound Publications has a proven devotion to quality, originality and integrity.

We are a small press with big ideas. As an independent publisher we strive to ensure that the mainstream is not the only stream. It is our intention at Homebound Publications to preserve contemplative storytelling. We publish full-length introspective works of creative non-fiction as well as essay collections, travel writing, poetry, and novels. In all our titles, our intention is to introduce new perspectives that will directly aid humankind in the trials we face at present as a global village.

WWW.HOMEBOUNDPUBLICATIONS.COM

CPSIA information can be obtained
at www.ICGtesting.com
Printed in the USA
FSOW02n0707211017
40022FS

9 781947 003705